ANIMAL PREDATORS
Polar Bears

SANDRA MARKLE

Carolrhoda Books, Inc. / Minneapolis

THE ANIMAL WORLD IS FULL OF
PREDATORS.

Predators are the hunters who find, catch, and eat other animals—their prey—in order to survive. Every environment has its chain of hunters. The smaller, slower, less able predators become prey for the bigger, faster, more cunning hunters. And everywhere, there are just a few kinds of predators at the top of the food chain. *In and around the ice-covered waters of the Arctic, one of these is the polar bear.*

Polar bears spend most of their lives hunting on the ice and in the frigid waters of the Arctic Ocean. They may swim as far as 60 miles (97 kilometers) without stopping, in their search for prey. Usually their prey is seals and small whales.

During the winter, large areas of the ocean are covered with an ice crust. In other places, this crust is broken into floating puzzle pieces, called ice floes. Polar bears are specially adapted to their hunting range on solid and broken ice.

A polar bear's coat is just the right color to make it hard for prey to see. The bear also has an extremely good sense of smell. It can hunt even in the middle of the Arctic winter, when it's dark nearly all of the time. In fact, a polar bear's sense of smell is so good it can smell prey from as far away as 20 miles (32 km).

The smell of seawater attracted this female polar bear across the ice. The open water is a breathing hole for a beluga whale. Seals and whales live in the sea, but they breathe air. Alone or in small groups, these animals work at keeping one or more spots free of ice throughout the Arctic winter.

As the polar bear nears the dark patch of open water, she sees the sleek body of a beluga whale. It sees her too and dives. The bear settles down beside the hole to wait. A beluga whale can hold its breath for about 15 minutes. But it must eventually surface to breathe. Finally, the whale returns, puffing a spout of water as it breathes through the blowhole (airhole) on top of its head.

The polar bear swipes one paw at the whale, trying to snag it with her strong, curved claws. But the whale escapes and dives underwater. The female bear plunges into the sea after it. The water is icy cold, but the bear's thick fur coat and 4-inch-thick (10-centimeter-thick) layer of fat keep her warm.

With another strong swipe of a big paw, she snags the whale's tail. Then the big bear sinks her teeth into the whale and climbs out onto the ice. The bear is almost 8 feet (more than 2 meters) long and weighs close to 500 pounds (225 kilograms). Even though the beluga whale is nearly as big as she is, the polar bear is able to drag it out onto the ice. There she quickly makes her kill. Minutes later, seagulls arrive to share the meal.

When the polar bear opens her mouth and growls, the birds fly away. The polar bear's main weapons are her forty-two sharp teeth. The teeth include four sharp canines that easily bite into the whale's tough skin. The rest of the bear's teeth work like scissors to slice off the chunks of skin and fat that she gulps down.

A polar bear needs to eat about 4 pounds (2 kg) of meat each day. But she may not catch food every day. So when she does, she eats a lot. In fact, a polar bear's stomach can hold about 20 percent of her body weight in food.

After she eats, the female polar bear rolls on the ice. It's her way to clean the grease and blood from her fur. Clean fur does a better job of keeping her body warm. Her fur coat is adapted for living in the Arctic and for hunting on the ice and in the ice-cold sea. The coat has two layers. A dense, woolly under layer is covered by oily, stiff outer hairs that shed water easily.

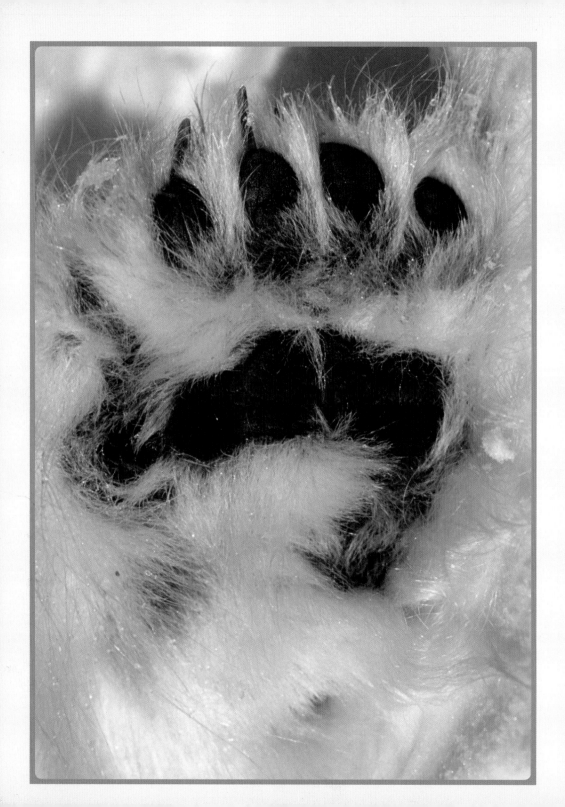

The female polar bear uses her teeth to pull chunks of ice from the hair covering the bottom of her paws. Even her feet are designed for hunting in the Arctic. Tufts of hair growing between her toes spread over her foot. The hair helps keep her from slipping when she walks across slick ice. Her black footpads are also covered by small, soft bumps that give her a good grip on the ice.

Now clean, the female polar bear lies down to sleep, saving energy for the next hunt. The bear's fur coat is made of many hollow, transparent hairs. These hairs let the sun's energy shine directly onto her black skin to warm it. The bear's thick coat keeps the warmth close to her body. On this sunny day, she heats up quickly. Soon she is so warm she needs to stretch out on the ice.

Day after day, the female polar bear uses the ice as a platform for hunting the animals living in the sea beneath her. Deep in the sea, the bearded seal is hunting too. It uses its big eyes to spot prey. When the seal sees a fish, it kicks with its hind flippers to surge ahead and catch the fish in its mouth. Finally, the seal needs to surface to breathe. So it returns to the hole it has chewed open in the ice.

The seal is nearly to the surface when it spots the bear's big head in its breathing hole. But it's too late. The female polar bear bites, sinking her teeth into the seal's neck.

Then the polar bear yanks the seal out onto the ice, biting again to make the kill. Since food is plentiful, the polar bear eats only her favorite parts of the seal—the skin and fat.

As the weeks pass, the Arctic days grow longer. By summer, the sun is shining nearly twenty-four hours each day. Then the ice crust cracks apart even more. The female polar bear leaps between the floating ice floes as though following a path of stepping-stones. Day-by-day, she must spend more time swimming while she hunts.

The female polar bear spots a ringed seal resting on an ice floe. She slides nose first into the icy sea and paddles hard with her front paws to pull herself underwater. The big bear swims toward the floe and only pokes up her black nose every few minutes to take a breath. Paddling with her front paws while steering with her hind legs, she sneaks up to the seal. The cautious seal frequently lifts its head to watch for predators.

Suddenly, the polar bear explodes from the water. But the seal already had spotted the predator and slipped into the sea. Since the seal can swim faster than the polar bear, it escapes easily. That day the bear goes hungry.

When most of the sea ice has melted, the female bear must go ashore to hunt. She hauls out onto Wrangel Island, off the coast of Russia. Walruses have come to the island too. Groups of them are resting on the beach. By staying close together, the walruses have many eyes and ears on the alert for predators.

The bear tries to stalk a female walrus and her calf. But the mother is alerted when nearby walruses hurry into the sea. She and her calf follow them. The polar bear doesn't chase after the calf because its mother would defend it. The adult walrus's tusks could easily give the bear a deep slash.

The big female bear plods slowly along the rocky beach. She sniffs the air for prey. But the island has fewer prey than the frozen sea.

Just over the crest of the hill, she encounters two male polar bears. It's the breeding season, and at six years old, the female is ready to mate for the first time. A fierce battle quickly breaks out as the two males fight for the chance to mate with her. Both suffer cuts and one loses a tooth before the stronger male wins. Then the female leads the winning male on a chase before stopping to mate.

After mating the female is on her own again. She needs to find food to build up the fat her body will need to carry her through the period when her cubs are developing. But food is scarce on shore and it's several days before the female polar bear finds any prey.

She finally finds a dead beluga whale that washed onto the beach. It's already been claimed by a young female polar bear. Young adult polar bears aren't as skilled at hunting as the bigger, older bears. They survive by finding and eating leftovers.

Holding her head down in her threat pose, the big female approaches the younger bear. The young polar bear abandons her meal and moves away. Then the big female digs into the remains of the whale.

Day after day, the female polar bear hunts and finds food where she can. Summer is the toughest hunting season for her. She heads out to sea as soon as the ice cover starts to form once again. But this year, as the days grow shorter and colder, she digs a den in the snow and goes to sleep. After about two months, she gives birth to two cubs. Each is no bigger than a soft-drink can.

At first, the cubs must depend on their mother for warmth and food.
Nursing frequently on their mother's rich milk, the cubs grow quickly.
They eat and sleep most of the day.

The cubs begin to play and explore. But they are still small enough to be prey for predators, such as wolf packs or even male polar bears. So whenever they are out of their den, their mother stays close by.

Once the cubs grow a little bigger, they leave the safety of the den for good. They go along with their mother when she hunts for food on the beach. A tug-of-war game with a walrus calf's remains is a tasty game. It's also an introduction to the food they'll be eating when they hunt on their own.

The cubs will continue to nurse for the next two years. They will also begin to share their mother's meals. They'll learn that dead whales that have washed ashore make easy eating.

The cubs will also learn how to hunt and catch prey by following their mother, watching her, and copying what they see her do. Finally, when the young bears are two to three years old, they will go off on their own. Then the frozen Arctic will have a new generation of polar bears on the hunt.

Looking Back

- Take another look at the polar bear on page 6. Like other big bears, this one has paws that are nearly 12 inches (30 cm) wide. Such big paws spread out her massive weight, helping to keep her from breaking through thin ice.

- Look through the book again, checking out the color of a polar bear's nose, lips, and the soles of its feet. Those are the only parts of the bear's skin that aren't covered by fur, so you can see that this white bear has black skin.

- Take another look at the polar bear on page 17. You may be surprised to learn that a polar bear's hind limbs are longer than its front legs. The bear's muscular hind end powers its leaps, like the leap on page 25.

- Did you notice how fat polar bears look? Polar bears look fat because of the thick layer of fat they have beneath their skin. When the bear is swimming in the icy ocean, this fat helps keep the bear's muscles and inner body from becoming chilled.

Glossary

ARCTIC OCEAN: the smallest ocean on Earth. It's mostly located north of the Arctic Circle and has an ice covering for much of the year.

CLAWS: hard nails about 2 inches (5 cm) long on the tips of toes that help a polar bear have traction as it walks and helps it hold onto its prey

ICE FLOE: a sheet of floating ice

PREDATOR: an animal that is a hunter

PREY: an animal that a predator catches to eat

SEAGULL: a web-footed, white or grayish bird that flies out to sea in search of food

SEAL: a meat-eating sea mammal adapted for living and hunting in the ocean

WALRUS: a large sea mammal with tough skin, feet flattened into flippers, and large tusks

WHALE: a large sea mammal that breathes through a blowhole (airhole) on top of its head and has front flippers and a flat horizontal tail

Further Information

BOOKS

Biel, Timothy Levi. *Polar Bears*. San Diego: Zoobooks / Wildlife Education, 1997. This book is packed with scientific facts about polar bears and activities that explore its unique habitat.

London, Jonathan. *Ice Bear and Little Fox*. New York: Dutton Books, 1998. Experience a young polar bear's first year on its own. This story also shares the life of the arctic fox who trails after the bear, living on its leftovers.

Markle, Sandra. *Growing Up Wild: Bears*. New York: Atheneum, 2000. Learn about the birth and development of young bears, including polar bears.

Patent, Dorothy Hinshaw. A *Polar Bear Biologist at Work*. Danbury, CT: Franklin Watts, 2002. This book brims with facts about polar bears and their habitat as shared by Chuck Jonkel, a field biologist with more than 40 years' experience studying bears.

————. *Polar Bears*. Photographs by William Muñoz. Minneapolis: Carolrhoda Books, Inc., 2000. Explore the life cycle and habits of polar bears.

VIDEOS

Polar Bear Alert (National Geographic, 1982). Examine the lives and behaviors of polar bears in the wild and close to people at Churchill, Manitoba, in Canada.

Index

For Ben and Rose Beckdahl, with love, as you begin your lives together

The author would like to thank the following persons for sharing their expertise and enthusiasm: Ian Stirling, Polar Bear Biologist, Canadian Wildlife Service, and Nikita Ovsyanikol, Senior Research Scientist and Head of Environmental Education Department for Wrangel Island State Nature Reserve, Member of IUCN Polar Bear Specialist Group. And a very special thanks to Skip Jeffery, for his help and support.

Photo Acknowledgments

The images in this book are used with the permission of: © Wayne Lynch, pp 1, 5; © Amos Nachoum/Seapics.com. p. 3; © Daniel J. Cox/naturalexposures.com, pp. 4, 13, 23; © Nikita Ovsyanikov, pp. 6, 26; © sue flood/naturepl.com, pp. 7, 8, 11; © Kenneth W. Fink/Bruce Coleman Inc., p. 10; © Kennan Ward/CORBIS, p. 14; © Flip Nicklin/Minden Pictures, pp 16, 18; © Thomas Mangelsen/Minden Pictures, p. 17; © Glenn Williams/Minden Pictures, pp. 20, 21; © Doug Allan/Oxford Scientific Films, p. 24; © Jim Brandenburg/Minden Pictures, p. 25; © Gary and Terry Andrewartha/SAL/Oxford Scientific Films, p. 29; © Bob and Clara Calhoun/Bruce Coleman, Inc, p. 30; © Norbert Rosing/Oxford Scientific Films, p 32; © Mitsuaki Iwago/Minden Pictures, pp. 33, 34; © Steven Kazlowski/Seapics.com, pp. 35, 36; © Galen Rowell/CORBIS, p. 37.

Cover: © Johnny Johnson/Animals Animals. Back cover: © Thomas Mangelsen/Minden Pictures.

Carolrhoda Books, Inc.
A division of Lerner Publishing Group
241 First Avenue North
Minneapolis, MN 55401 U.S.A.

Website address: www.lernerbooks.com

Library of Congress Cataloging-in-Publication Data

Markle, Sandra.
    Polar bears / by Sandra Markle.
        p.   cm.—(Animal predators)
    Summary: Describes the physical characteristics, behavior, habitat, and life cycle of the polar bear.
    Includes bibliographical references (p. 39) and index.
    ISBN: 1—57505—730—1 (lib. bdg. : alk. paper)
    1. Polar bear—Juvenile literature. [1. Polar bear. 2. Bears.] I. Title II. Series: Markle, Sandra. Animal predators.
    QL737.C27M3453 2004
    599.786—dc22   2003019515

Manufactured in the United States of America
1 2 3 4 5 6 — DP — 09 08 07 06 05 04